Led by the Spirit

Into the Consciousness of Christ

Dennis J. Billy, C.Ss.R.

En Route Books and Media, LLC
St. Louis, MO

⊕*ENROUTE*
Make the time

En Route Books and Media, LLC
5705 Rhodes Avenue
St. Louis, MO 63109

Cover credit: Sebastian Mahfood

ISBN-13: 978-1-952464-92-8
Library of Congress Control Number:
2021943390

Contents

Introduction

Following Jesus means being open to and led by his Spirit. This book explores the meaning of this phrase by looking at the larger picture of why God entered our world and became one of us in the first place. It hinges on one fundamental insight. If the mystery of the Incarnation marks the beginning of a renewed friendship between God and man, then the sending of his Spirit reveals an even deeper way for the two of them to relate. Because of the Spirit, God is able to dwell within the human heart throughout the corridors of history.

The God of Love hatched this plan for us from all eternity. Love, by its very nature, is self-diffusive. That is to say that it seeks to extend itself freely to others. God created the world we live in, redeemed us, and now seeks to sanctify us—all out of love. By creating us in his image and likeness, he enabled us to enter into a relationship with him and now wishes to share his very life with us. He became one of us so that our humanity might mingle with his, thus enabling us to share in his divinity. The Spirit living within us is the means by which this process of divinization takes place. Jesus sent us his Spirit, in other words, to be present to us in an even more intimate way than when he walked the earth two millennia ago. He wanted not merely to enter our world as he did then but also to explore the interior landscape of our souls and live within our hearts.

The book has five chapters, each of which focuses on a different aspect of life in the Spirit. Chapter one, "Jesus, the New Adam," looks at the Spirit's sanctifying role in the New Creation that resulted from the Father's creation of the world and the Son's redemption of its fallen nature. Chapter two, "Jesus in Our Midst," listens to the groaning of the Spirit within our hearts that helps us sense the hidden presence of the Lord both within ourselves and in others. Chapter three, "Walking by Faith," considers the life of prayer that enables us to sense the Spirit's promptings in our lives and enjoy his manifold fruits. Chapter four, "Practicing the Presence of God," examines the various ways we can live in the present moment and be sensitive to the presence of the Spirit in our lives. Chapter five, "All the Way to Heaven," discusses the nature of our spiritual journey and the Spirit's role in helping us reach of final destination. Each chapter ends with a series of reflection questions and a heartfelt prayer to the Spirit for guidance during our earthly sojourn. The book ends with some concluding remarks and a list of other books I have authored for those interested in the spiritual life and the ways of the Spirit.

Even though the Spirit is like the wind and blows where it wills (Jn 3:8), he does not force itself on anyone and, for this reason, refuses to trespass on the dry, deserted landscape of a closed-in, stony heart. To be open to and led by the Spirit means that we view life through the eyes of faith, walk in hope, and live our lives for the love of God and neighbor. It also means that we seek to live in the present moment and practice living in God's presence by being sensitive to and following the promptings of his Spirit. As the bond between the Father and the Son, the Spirit fosters unity rather than division, peace rather than discord, deep inner joy rather than isolation and loneliness. We pray to the Spirit to show us how to love during our pilgrimage on earth and to ask for the strength to pick up our cross daily in the following of Christ. If nothing else, this little book seeks to be a source of comfort to everyone trying to walk the way of holiness, find their way to God, and sense his presence, the presence of the kingdom, in their midst: "Come, Holy Spirit, fill the hearts of your faithful and enkindle in them the fire of your love." May these and similar words be ever on our lips.

Chapter One

Jesus, the New Adam

The credibility of the Christian religion rests on the belief that Jesus' resurrection from the dead actually happened. As St. Paul writes, "... if Christ has not been raised, then our proclamation has been in vain and your faith has been in vain" (1 Cor 15:14).[1] His resurrection, according to Catholic doctrine, was not merely a symbol, indicating that his life somehow continued after his burial in the tomb, or some mythic expression of humanity's deepest existential hopes, but an actual event that occurred in time and space, yet also transcended them. It was, in other words,

---

[1] Unless otherwise stated, all Scripture quotations come from *Holy Bible: New Revised Standard Version with Apocrypha* (New York: Oxford University Press, 1989).

a historical event with transhistorical consequences. If this is true, then our belief in Jesus' resurrection has ramifications for the way we view the world and our place in it.

Jesus, we believe, is the New Adam (1 Cor 15:45), who heralded the dawn of a New Creation (2 Cor 5:17). The Eucharist he instituted is the sacrament of this New Creation and its celebration represents the rising of the Risen Lord within our hearts. St. Paul makes this clear when he writes, ".... It is no longer I who live, but it is Christ who lives in me" (Gal 2:29). The whole purpose of Jesus' resurrection was not merely to heal a broken and fragmented humanity of the wounds it had inflicted on itself and on all creation as a result of Adam's tragic fall from grace, but to elevate it to new heights by entering into the world he created and transforming it from the inside-out. To understand the nature of this transformation, we need to understand the relationship between divine being and divine action.

Our Creative, Redemptive, & Sanctifying God

Christians believe that God is an intimate unity of three Persons in one God—Father, Son, and Spirit—all of whom mutually co-inhere while maintaining their distinct identities.[2] Their unity and multiplicity are thoroughly integrated, so much so that to separate their multiple identities from their metaphysical unity would be a distortion of the mystery of love they represent. Since action flows from being, it follows that God's actions flow from his Triune makeup. This truth is represented by the Christian belief that, while God always acts as one, each of his three loving actions outside himself (his so-

---

[2] The official term for the interpenetration of the Three Persons of the Blessed Trinity is *perichoresis* (in Greek) and *circumincessio* (in Latin). The term "coinherence" comes from Charles Williams, *The Descent of the Dove: A Short History of the Holy Spirit in the Church* (London: Faber and Faber, 1939), 234-36.

called *ad extra* economic activities) are typically associated with one of the Persons of the Trinity: Creation with the Father, Redemption with the Son, and Sanctification with the Holy Spirit. Because he acts as both one and many, at one and the same time, God can be said to have left an imprint of his Trinitarian existence in each of these activities. There is, in other words, a reflection of the Trinity in each of his creative, redemptive, and sanctifying activities.

In the act of creation, for example, God made humanity in his image (Gn 1:27) and left vestiges (or signs) of his presence in the rest of his creation. In the act of redemption, moreover, the mystery of the Incarnation and of Christ's passion, death, and resurrection flows from the intimate union of will between the Father and the Son, a union which itself is the love of the Holy Spirit within God himself and toward the whole of creation. In the act of humanity's sanctification, the transformation of the world by the power of the Spirit takes place only because this same Spirit is nothing but the intimate love between the Father and the Son. What is more, each of these Trinitarian activities takes place both in time, throughout time, and beyond time. Creation, in other words, is *guttatim* ("drop-by-drop): God creates, is creating, and will continue to create until the consummation of the world at the end of time. The same can be said for the actions of redemption and humanity's sanctification: we have been redeemed; we are being redeemed; and we will be redeemed. Similarly, we have been sanctified by virtue of our immersion in the baptismal waters; we are being sanctified by the presence of the Holy Spirit in our lives; and we will be sanctified and made fully holy when we enter God's presence and see him face-to-face.

If the intimate relations of the Three Persons of the Blessed Trinity are reflected in their creative, redemptive, and sanctifying actions toward humanity and the world we inhabit, it also follows that these three actions are themselves intimately related. The Father's creative activity, in other words, already contains within itself a foretaste of the Son's redemptive and the Spirit's sanctifying activities. Christ's redemptive action, moreover, presupposes Father's creative activity and anticipates the sanctifying action of the Spirit, whose work, in turn, represents the culmination of God's creative and redemptive activity. The mutual coinherence of God's immanent (*ad intra*) relations reflected in his external (*ad extra*) actions offers a key to understanding our relationship to Jesus and our place in the New Creation, heralded in by his resurrection from the dead.

Our Lord's resurrection presupposes the mystery of the Incarnation, the belief that God decided to heal the world gone awry through Adam's fall from grace by entering our world, becoming human, and sacrificing himself for our sake, so that through his death and resurrection, we ourselves might one day conquer death, share in his divine life, and become inhabitants of a New Creation. His resurrection, moreover, requires us to understand how the principle of coinherence, which helps us understand the mystery of Love within the Trinity, also extends to the relationship between Christ's human and divine natures. That is to say that, in a way similar to the Three Persons of the Blessed Trinity, the human and divine natures of Jesus interpenetrate one another, while remaining mutually distinct and separate. Jesus' humanity, in other words, penetrates his divinity—and vice versa. What is more, to understand our relationship to Jesus the New Adam, the firstborn of the New Creation, we need to understand our relationship to the Old Adam, the firstborn of the Old Creation.

Adam and the Fall: The Old Creation

The Hebrew word, *'ādām*, can refer either to humanity as a whole or a single person. In the context of the creation story in Genesis, it seems to refer to both.[3] If God created us in his image and likeness, it follows that we would consist of a singular plurality and plural singularity, just as can be found in God. If this be so, then there must have been some sort of collective consciousness that united the first man and woman with their offspring. Note that the first man and woman came into existence when God breathed into their evolutionary forebearers a rational soul. The physical evolution of the human race must therefore be distinguished from the coming into existence of the first human person in whom God infused a rational (as opposed to an animal or vegetative) soul. The anthropological makeup of the first human beings thus had five intimately related dimensions: the physical, the psychological

---

[3] *The Catholic Study Bible*, Donald Senior, John J. Collins, Mary Ann Getty eds. 2d ed. (New York: Oxford University, 2011), 12 (note to Gn 1:26).

(mental), the spiritual, the social, and a collective consciousness.

On the physical level, human beings had material bodies, which enabled them to interact with and watch over the world around them. On the psychological level, they were able to think, will, remember, imagine, feel, and interpret what they were experiencing. On the spiritual level, they could stand in awe at the beauty of creation, sense that there was something beyond the present world, and live in close communion with God, their Creator. On the social level, they were able to interact with one another, raise families, and supply the basic building blocks of human civilization. On the level of collective consciousness, they shared a common awareness that enabled them to work in unison with one another, while at the same time living as free individuals. In this instance, we might say that the principle of coinherence operated in humanity in such a way that individuals existed in the collectivity—and vice versa.

The world of nature gives us some insight into how the individual and collective can work together at one and the same time. We need only to look at a colony of ants, observe a hive of bees at work, watch a flock of birds in flight, or read about the hidden life of trees to see that the individual and collective are not mutually exclusive, but can work in harmony to produce something greater than either can ever possibly achieve alone. The Augustinian concept of a seminal nature existing in our first parents also reflects this understanding of the intimate connection between the individual and the collective whole. The Jungian concept of the collective unconscious, moreover, points to a remnant of what was once a fully ablaze collective awareness shared by all of humanity. These insights have important ramifications for our understanding of humanity's fall from grace.

The Christian doctrine of the Fall claims that somewhere at the dawn of our existence, humanity in both its collective and individual dimensions disobeyed God's commands and deviated from the path he had designed for it. The Genesis account says that man was free to live in the Garden, walk in fellowship with God, and exercise stewardship over the goods of creation. Adam and Eve were told they could eat of all the trees in the Garden save one: that of the knowledge of good and evil (Gn 3:1-5). Tempted by the serpent, who tells her that she would become like God if she ate this fruit, Eve eats of the fruit and convinces her husband to do the same. This sin of disobedience is typically interpreted as one of pride, a desire to put themselves in the place of God and decide for themselves what is good and evil, thereby placing themselves at the center of the moral universe. Once done, the resulting fall from grace had great repercussions for all of humanity and, because we are the pinnacle of God's creation, the rest of the created order.

On the anthropological level, humanity fell from grace on each of the five dimensions listed earlier. As a result of the Fall: "We have lost God's friendship. We feel alienated from ourselves, others, and creation. Our minds have become enfeebled. Our wills have been weakened. Our passions and emotions have become disordered. We experience work as a burden. We become ill and suffer disease of every kind. We become feeble with time and age without grace. We encounter death, are afraid of it, and dread its coming."[4] Worse yet, we lost touch with our collective consciousness, as it fragmented into a number of smaller social units that saw each other as potential threats to their well-being and began warring with one another. The loss of our collective human consciousness, which previously had sustained a sense of unity across the whole of human existence, caused

---

[4] Dennis J. Billy, "Faith, Conscience, and the Threefold Way," in *Contemplating the Future of Moral Theology: Essays in Honor of Brian V. Johnstone*, Robert C. Koerpel and Vimal Tirimana (Eugene, OR: Pickwick, 2017), 6.

these smaller social units (clans, tribes, kinsmen) to contend with one another and vie for dominance. The stories in Genesis of Cain and Abel (Gn 4:1-16), Lamech (Gn 4:23-24), Noah and the Flood (Gn 6:5-9:29), the Tower of Babel (Gn 11:1-9), and Sodom and Gomorrah (Gn 19:1-29) reflect this fragmentation of the collective whole that occurred as a result of the Fall. Still worse, the sin of Adam and Eve caused tremendous spiritual turmoil within the human soul, for they and their progeny were cast out of Paradise, lost their intimate fellowship with God, and lived in a contentious relationship with the rest of the created world by becoming its exploiters rather than the stewards that God had originally intended us to be.

The New Adam and Redemption: The New Creation

Jesus is the New Adam. He came to make all things new (Rev 21:5). He entered our

world (in the mystery of his Incarnation),
gave himself to us completely (in the mystery
of his passion and death), to become nourishment for us (in the mystery of the Eucharist)
and a source of hope for us (in the mysteries
of his Resurrection and Ascension into
Heaven). He did all this to set right our
humanity and the world gone awry as a result
of Adam's fall. As the New Adam, Jesus' historical presence in space and time presupposes the historical presence of the Old
Adam, our first parent. Because the Old
Adam possessed both an individual and collective consciousness, the same must be true
of the New Adam. What is more, Mary, the
mother of Jesus and the Church, is often de-
picted as the New Eve. As the first of all
human beings to experience the fullness as
redemption, she parallels the figure of Eve,
the mother of all humanity, who was the first
to eat of the tree of the knowledge of good
and evil and thereby forfeit her life of fellowship with God and the right to live in Para-

dise. Jesus, the New Adam, and Mary, the New Eve, herald in the New Creation. Their obedience to the will of the Father offsets the disobedience of our first parents and allows the wounds sustained by the Fall to be healed and ultimately transformed into something higher and more elevated than it was before. The consequences of this wonderful mystery of Redemption are startling.

To begin with, the collective awareness of humanity, lost as a result of Adam's fall from grace, was regained by means of Jesus's resurrection. His rising from the dead signifies not merely the glorification of his own personal humanity, but also that of the entire human race, both the living and the dead. Jesus' resurrection gave rise to a new humanity, one in which the coinherence between the personal and the communal, the individual and the collective remained intact. As the Apostle Paul reminds us, "For just as the body is one and has many members, and all the members of the body, though many, are one body, so it is with Christ" (1 Cor 12:12). More than mere metaphor, this insight reveals a very deep truth about the nature of the risen Lord. Through baptism, we participate in a very real way in Jesus' death and resurrection. As Paul says, "But if we have died with Christ, we believe that we will also live with him" (Rom 6:8).

This new life takes place not only at some future point but also in the present life by virtue of the indwelling of the Holy Spirit. Through his Spirit, Jesus wishes to take possession of our souls and incorporate us in a very real and palpable way into his risen and glorified life. He does so, however, not by taking control of our individual minds and hearts but by maintaining a very fine balance between the individual and the collective whole, one that preserves individual freedom while at the same time allowing it to live out of the larger collective of the New Adam made possible by Christ's resurrection. Because we are members of his Mystical

Body, we ourselves are members of the New Adam. Christ, in other words, rises not only from the tomb, but also from within our stony hearts, turning them not merely into natural hearts, but now able to participate in his divinized, supernatural heart. As Athanasius of Alexandria notes, "God became man so that man might become divine."[5] Because the Son of God became a man, we are able to share in his divinity. This intimate human-and-divine sharing enables us to retain our own personal identities but, at the same time, participate in the collective whole of Jesus, the New Adam. It enables us to think, feel, remember, imagine, pray, and act as Jesus does. As St. Paul states, "As many of you as were baptized into Christ have clothed yourselves with Christ" (Gal 3:27). Our baptism *into* Christ means that in him that "we live and move and have our being" (Acts 17:

---

[5] Athanasius of Alexandria, *De incarnatione* 54.3.

28). The Catholic doctrine of the communion of saints in heaven is a wonderful expression of this participation in the collective consciousness of Christ. Those of us who are pilgrims on the way yearn for the day when our humanity will be so completely transformed by the movement of the Spirit in our lives that we, too, will partake fully in this collective consciousness of Jesus, the New Adam, our risen and glorious Lord.

In addition to reestablishing our collective consciousness and incorporating it into his risen and glorious humanity, Jesus' resurrection from the dead has many other consequences that impact our lives. Through it: "He reestablishes our friendship with God. He heals our relationship with ourselves, others, and God. He renews our minds. He strengthens our wills. He orders our passions and emotions. He helps us find meaning and joy in our work. He accompanies us in our suffering and heals us in due time. He is present to us at all stages of our lives. He gives us courage to face death and look beyond it."[6] He accomplishes these things in our personal lives so that we can ultimately share in the collective consciousness that he shares with the communion of saints and ultimately with all the members of his Mystical Body. Because of Jesus, the New Adam, we are members of this glorified collective whole. This communal consciousness is divinized and goes far beyond that shared by our early ancestors. What they shared on a natural level has now been elevated by grace and allowed to share in the very consciousness and life of God himself. It is interesting to note that what caused Adam and Eve to fall from grace (their desire to be like God) is itself freely bestowed on them through Christ's paschal mystery. It is also interesting to note that, because of this divinized collective consciousness, the risen and glorified

---

[6] Billy, "Faith, Conscience, and the Threefold Way," 12.

Christ was able to move through space and time in a way that enabled him to be in multiple places at once, go through doors and walls, keep his identity hidden from others, eat and drink with his disciples, and live in the hearts of his followers. When seen in this light, the Easter proclamation, "He is Risen!" pertains not merely to Jesus' body and soul rising from the empty tomb, but also his rising and living within the hearts of those who believe in him and experience him in the breaking of the bread.

Conclusion

What can we say by way of conclusion? The Three Persons of the Blessed Trinity interpenetrate each other and do so while maintaining their separate identities in the midst of their intimate metaphysical unity. Since action flows from being, the one God of Father, Son, and Spirit, acts in a manner commensurate with his coinhering nature. While he always acts as one, his three *ad extra* (economic) loving actions are typically associated with one of the Persons: Creation with the Father, Redemption with the Son, and Sanctification with the Holy Spirit.

Because of his coinhering nature, God leaves behind his Trinitarian imprint in all he does: he creates us in his image and likeness; he redeems us by uniting himself to our human nature in a coinhering (hypostatic) manner; he sanctifies us by allowing his Spirit—the bond between the Father and the Son—to dwell within our hearts and transform us from within. This inner change is the basis for the ultimate transformation of humanity and the world we inhabit. Humanity's wounds caused by the disobedience to God's will on the part of our first parents are tended to, healed, and ultimately elevated by virtue of Jesus' obedience to the Father's will, which culminated in his death on the cross and his being raised by the Father on the third day.

Because of this obedience, Jesus is the
New Adam, the New Man, the Alpha and the
Omega, the First and the Last. He was sent by
the Father to redeem the world so that he
could impart his Spirit to sanctify us and
world we inhabit. By entering our world, he
redeemed humanity's fallen nature and
raised it to new heights. He did so by taking
on our human nature, thus giving us a chance
to unite ourselves with his divinity and share
in the intimate love of the Trinity. Our sharing in the divine life has concrete repercussions for the new humanity by virtue of
being members of Jesus' New Man, his Mystical Body. Because of him, we have regained
the collective consciousness lost as a result of
Adam's fall from grace, a consciousness
which has now become divinized by virtue of
its being rooted in the mind and heart of the
glorified and risen Lord. Our participation in
this collective consciousness is itself a sign of
the renewed friendship we share with God,
which has also resulted in the enlightening of

our minds, the strengthening of our wills, the taming of our passions, and the ultimate renewal of our material existence. In the end, it is important to note that Jesus could become the New Adam only because of the humble *fiat* of his mother, Mary, who embraced God's will for herself as Jesus, her Son, embraced the Father's will for himself by embracing his sacrificial death on the cross unreservedly and without complaint. The disobedience of Adam and Eve, our first parents, was thus offset by the obedience of Jesus and Mary, the New Adam and the New Eve. To them, we owe everything. It is them whom we follow, whom we seek in our midst, and in whom we hope one day to experience the fullness of redemption.

Led by the Spirit

What is your understanding of God's action in the world? Do you view him as a God of Love who created the world you inhabit, redeemed it, and is now in the process of sanctifying it? To what extent are these actions related to the Christian doctrine of humanity's fall from grace? In what ways are they independent of it? What were some of the consequences of this fall from grace? Do you believe that the collective awareness of our ancestors became badly fragmented as a result of the fall? If so, do you believe it can be restored? If so, how so? In what ways is Jesus the New Adam? In what ways is Mary the New Eve? How have they healed humanity's wounded nature? How have they repaired its corporate consciousness? How have they transformed it? What role has the Holy Spirit played in God's providential plan for humanity?

Prayer to the Holy Spirit

Come, Holy Spirit, bless me with a deep awareness of your transforming presence. Help me to open my heart to your sanctifying grace. Help me to get in touch with my deep, inner wounds and reveal them to the Lord. Have his healing hand touch them and make them whole. Open my mind and my heart to sense your quiet promptings. Help me to respond to them without a moment's hesitation. Come, Holy Spirit, come. Bless me with your manifold gifts and fruits. Mary, my mother, woman filled with the grace of the Spirit, pray for me.

Chapter Two

Jesus in Our Midst

Jesus Christ, the Alpha and Omega, the beginning and the end, came to make all things new. God's entrance into the world he created by taking on human nature and becoming one of us marks the beginning of a new era for humanity and the world it inhabits. Because we are part of God's creation, the mystery of the Incarnation has ramifications not just for us but for everything around us. If Adam and Eve's fall from grace has affected all of creation, then the remedy of the Redemption not only reverses that trend but also elevates the original created order to new heights.

This New Creation far exceeds the order in the created world originally established by

God. Since "grace perfects nature,"[7] the out-pouring of Christ's redemptive grace on the world not only heals it of its wounds but also raises it to a new level, one that allows the entire created order to share in the divine life itself. God became man not only to divinize humanity, but also so that the entire created order could participate in varying degrees in his divine life. Paul proclaims in the Acts of the Apostles, "In him we live and move and have our being" (Acts 17:28), which holds true not merely for humanity but for all creation.

God's recreative action of making all things new does not happen all at once. As the Scriptures tells us, "… with the Lord one day is like a thousand years, and a thousand years are like one day" (2 Pet 3:8). Inaugurated by the mysteries of the Incarnation and Christ's passion, death, and resurrection, this

---

[7] Thomas Aquinas, *Quaestiones quodlibetales*, 4. 6.

action is still unfolding in our midst. The Eucharist, the Sacrament of the New Creation, which changes bread and wine, the work of human hands, into the body and blood of Our Lord, represents the first fruits of this gentle, unobtrusive process. For the most part, this quiet transformation takes place in our midst, but in a hidden way. It begins with the movement of the Holy Spirit within our hearts and can be seen only through the eyes of faith. As the Apostle Paul asserts "… we walk by faith, not by sight" (2 Cor 5:7). Only if we seek to experience reality through the eyes of faith can we ever hope to find Jesus in our midst and God's presence in all things. Jesus himself tells us, "Do you have eyes, and fail to see? Do you have ears, and fail to hear?" (Mk 8:18). If only we could look at the world around us through the eyes of faith, then we would sense the presence of God's kingdom taking shape in our hearts and in our very midst as well.

All Creation Groans

When he taught his disciples how to pray,
Jesus himself included the petition "Your
kingdom come," (Mt 6:10), even though his
very presence among them meant that this
kingdom was also already in their midst. This
"already-but-not-yet" character of the New
Creation creates a sense of anticipation and
expectant hope. St. Augustine of Hippo's
famous words in the opening chapter of his
Confessions remind us of our intense yearning for him and the fullness of our redemption: "Thou hast made us for Thyself, O Lord,
and our heart is restless until it finds its rest
in Thee."[8] The Apostle Paul also points out
that this intense sense of yearning for the fulfillment of things to come takes place within
all creation: "We know that the whole creation has been groaning in labor pains until
now; and not the creation but we ourselves,

---

[8] Augustine of Hippo, *Confessions*, 1.1

who have the first fruits of the Spirit, groan inwardly while we wait for adoption, the redemption of our bodies" (Rom 8:22-23). That same Spirit cries out within our hearts, "Abba, Father" (Rom 8:15; Gal 4:6), reminding us that we are no longer slaves to sin and decay but adopted sons and daughters of the Father. God looks upon us as he does his own Son, Jesus, the King of the New Creation and Prince of Peace. Since, as members of his body, we share in the noble heritage of God's Only Begotten Son, the sufferings of the present world pale in comparison to the glory that is to come (Rom 8:18).

This yearning within our hearts and all creation comes from the Spirit and is itself also a sign of God's intense longing for us. "The paradise of God," we are told, "is the heart of man."[9] Heaven, for him, is to dwell

---

[9] Alphonsus de Liguori, *The Way to Converse Always and Familiarly with God*, 1 in *Four Treatises on the Interior Life from St. Alphonsus Liguori* (Mesa, AZ: Scriptoria Books, 2011), 7.

within our hearts and experience his handi-work from the inside-out. His presence with-in our hearts is meant to spill over into our relationships with our family, friends, neigh-bors, community, nation, world, and to reach out to members of difference ethnic and cul-tural backgrounds, other religions, strangers, enemies, and ultimately all creation. The full-ness of the New Creation will come when this process of making all things new has come to term.

Christ's second coming will be a work of his Spirit and come from the New Creation itself, as it reaches maturity in the fullness of time, as the Mystical Body of Christ, the New Adam, achieves its full stature in the created order and mirrors completely the glorified presence he presently enjoys at the right hand of the Father. When seen in this light, Jesus' prayer for his disciples, "Father, protect them in your name that you have given me, so that they may be one, as we are one" (Jn 17:11), represents a heartfelt longing for their communion with God himself, as well as the New Creation they proclaim.

What can we take from all of this? In the end, there is a two-fold longing in our faith experience: our yearning for God and his yearning for us. This longing (groaning, we might say) permeates all of reality and is itself a sign of God's hidden presence in the human heart and in all creation. The question arises, however: How can we become more attuned to this yearning of the Spirit within us and in the world around us? How, in other words, can we become more sensitized to the promptings of the Spirit in our lives and do so in such a way that we are more in touch with his movement in the world around us? The answer to this question is as mysterious as the Spirit himself and the intimate mystery of Love in which he shares.

Our Revealing and Hidden God

While the God of Love holds everything in being from one moment to the next and is present everywhere by virtue of his creative power, in the New Creation inaugurated by Christ's redemptive sacrifice and the Spirit's sanctifying action, he is also present in a way that is, at one and the same time, both visible and hidden. Jesus is the concrete, visible expression of God's only begotten Son, who walked this earth some 2,000 years ago, taught in our midst, and performed many signs wonders before us. He is the God who became man, the Word made flesh, the Son of God and the Son of Man, someone like us who embraced his own death so that we might live. There is also something hidden and mysterious about Jesus, something that tells us that he is more than a man, more than a prophet, more than even the deepest dreams of the people of Israel. He is the Messiah, the Son of David, who is also the

King of Kings, the Prince of Peace, and the
Son of the Father. His relationship with the
Father is unique in all the world, yet all so
very hidden and mysterious. He and the
Father are one (Jn 10:30), and nothing will
ever separate them, not even death, which he
freely embraced so that we might share in his
intimate relationship with the Father.

The Catholic tradition has a way of deal-
ing with the visible and hidden presences of
our mysterious Triune God. It speaks of the
way of positive and negative theology, also
known respectively as the cataphatic and
apophatic ways. The differences between
these two approaches are most telling. The
former makes positive assertions about God
by means of words, images, and concepts,
while the latter states that God is ultimately
unknowable and that the closest we will ever
come to knowing what God is like is by
stating what God is not. The former represents the way of knowing; the latter, the way
of unknowing. One promotes the ability to

express the meaning of reality; the other embraces silence as the best way of reverencing our unknown God. The theologian most noted for exploring both of these approaches to talking about God is the Pseudo-Dionysius, who was most likely an early sixth-century Syrian monk writing under the pseudonym of Dionysius the Areopagite, the convert of St. Paul in Acts 17:34. While his *The Divine Names* focuses on the positive images and concepts we use to refer to God, his *Mystical Theology* emphasizes the way of negation.[10] One explores the possibilities of the way of knowing; the other, those of unknowing. Although the two approaches, he believed, complement each other, he understood that there was an infinite distance between whatever positive expressions we make of God and the actual reality of God's hidden

---

[10] See *Pseudo-Dionysius: The Complete Works*, trans. Colm Luibheid, The Classics of Western Spirituality (New York: Paulist, 1987), 47-141.

essence. That is to say that, even though God can reveal himself through words and images, he will always remain essentially unknowable (beyond description) to the finite human mind.

By employing each of these approaches in its approach to theology, the Catholic tradition preserves the sense of a God who, at one and the same time, reveals himself to us through word and sacrament, yet also remains mysteriously hidden from view. This delicate juxtaposition of the cataphatic and apophatic ways allows the Church to make a number of enigmatic statements about God's very nature. The Christian God is a sacramental God who shows himself to us in history through concrete, visible signs, yet remains strangely hidden from sight. He is a God who is simultaneously transcendent, incarnate, and immanent. He reveals himself through Scripture and the sacraments yet remains mysteriously hidden from plain view. In the Eucharist, for example, he reveals himself to the worshiping community by having his Word proclaimed, broken open, and shared, and actually enters our midst when the bread and wine which, once consecrated, are transformed into the body and blood of the Risen Lord. Still, God is both seen and unseen. On the strictly empirical level, nothing out of the ordinary happens during Mass: people gather; words are spoken; bread and wine shared; people depart. When seen through the eyes of faith, however, something very extraordinary is taking place: Christ's mystical body, the Church, renders worship to the Father; God's Word is spoken by the priest or deacon and touches the hearts of the faithful; God enters our midst and transforms chronological time (*Chronos*) into sacred time (*Kairos*); Christ's sacrificial death on Calvary, becomes mysteriously present in an unbloody way; bread and wine are themselves transformed into the body and blood of Jesus' glorified body; those who receive him are nourished spiritually and enter into Holy Communion with their Lord and Savior. The Eucharist is known as the "Sacrament of Sacraments," from the Latin word *sacramentum*, which translates the Greek *musterion*, meaning "mystery." Christians believe in a God conceals as much as he reveals—and vice versa.

Jesus in Our Midst

If grace perfects nature, as classical Catholic theology maintains, then we can say that God exists in the New Creation not only by virtue of his power, vestiges, and image, but also in his hidden presence which he reveals (yet also conceals) through the Church, Christ's Mystical Body, and her sacraments. Since these various kinds of presence can only be seen through the eyes of faith, it follows that Christians will find God both within themselves and in their midst only if they walk by faith as they journey through life and seek to enter into an intimate relationship with him. Because faith is itself a gift, and since it is intimately tied to the other theological virtues of hope and love, it follows that this great variety of presences in the New Creation are themselves signs that the spiritual life is not so much about our finding God, but of God's finding us. We find God in all things first and foremost by humbly recognizing how we ourselves have been gifted by God with the faith that he actually exists, the hope that we will one day see him face-to-face, and the love that empowers us to keep his word, do his will, and follow his commands, the most important of which is the new commandment he gave to his followers: "I give you a new commandment, that you love one another. Just as I have loved you, you also should love one another" (Jn 13:34).

How did Jesus love us? How did he demonstrate his unconditional love for fallen humanity? To what lengths did he go to show us the extent of the Father's love for us? The Gospel message proclaimed by his earliest disciples makes this very clear. He entered our world, gave himself to us completely, to become nourishment for us, and a source of hope for us. As his followers, we are called to do the same. Like him, we are called to enter the world of those around us, not only those closest to us, but also those who are strangers to us, marginalized, distant, and even at odds with us, even our enemies. Like him, we are called to give ourselves to others completely by sharing our lives with them, even to the point of dying for them. Like him, we are called to become nourishment for them. Like him, we are to be a source of hope them. The mysteries of the Incarnation and Jesus' passion, death, and resurrection are being dramatically played out in the lives of his followers, all of whom, are members of his Mystical Body, the Church. Jesus, the New Adam, does more than merely inspire his followers to live as he lived. Through the Church and her sacraments, he actually in-corporates them into himself. They become members of his corporate personality and share in the new collective consciousness of the new humanity. We are God's people. We belong to one another more than we will ever know. Because we are his children, the eyes of faith help us to see that, when all is said and done, we are all related to one another: we are all adopted sons and daughters of the Father.

In the end, we are able to find God in all things by clothing ourselves with Christ and sharing in his consciousness. The Apostle Paul tells us time and again in his letters to put on Christ, clothe ourselves with him, and to be of the same mind as him (Rom 13:14; Gal 3:27; Col 3:12). When we do this, a process occurs that is much more than mere pretending. In his book *Mere Christianity*, C. S. Lewis tells the story "about someone who had to wear a mask; a mask which made him look much nicer than he really was. He had to wear it for years. And when he took it off, he found his own face had grown to fit it. He was now really beautiful. What had begun as disguise had become reality."[11] A movement some years back tells a similar story. People were told to wear wristbands with the letters "WWJD?"—standing for "What would Jesus do?" The idea was that by trying to think and act like Jesus, we would over time, and through our cooperation with God's grace, actually begin to think and act as Jesus himself. Remember, "Grace perfects nature." Our desire to be like Christ opens the door of our hearts to the grace of the Holy Spirit. When we try to be like him, Jesus works with our desire (itself a movement of both mind and heart) and uses it to gradually transform us in a way that allows us to participate in his consciousness. Putting on the mind of Christ, in other words, ultimately leads us to sharing in the consciousness of Christ himself and finding him both with our hearts and in our

---

[11] C. S. Lewis, *Mere Christianity* (New York: Macmillan, 1952), 160.

midst. All of this has its consequences in the life of the believer (Phil 2:5).

The Friends of God

The martyrs of the early Church and the saints of late antiquity were known as the "friends of God."[12] They were the ones who were so successful in "putting on the mind of Christ," of "taking off the old self and putting on the new," that they eventually came to think and act and live as Jesus did. They befriended Jesus and he, in turn, befriended them. In doing so, they were not afraid of giving witness to him. So, closely linked were their lives to his that they were even willing to lay down their lives for him. So intimately were they united to him in faith that he was now living out his life, death, and resurrection through them. What the Apostle Paul

[12] Peter Brown, *The Making of Late Antiquity* (Cambridge, MA: Harvard University, 1978), 54-80.

affirmed so many years before about himself (Gal 2:20) applies equally well to them: it was no longer they who were living but Christ who was living in them.

The early saints and martyrs had become, in effect, other christs and through their witness unto death were nourishment for others. In his "Letter to the Romans," Ignatius of Antioch shows how his giving witness to Christ unto death becomes bread for others: "I am the wheat of God and am ground by the teeth of the wild beasts, that I may be found the pure bread of Christ."[13] A similar Eucharistic theme is related in *The Martyrdom of Polycarp*. The bishop of Smyrna, who was being burned at the stake, "… appeared within not like flesh which is burnt, but as bread that is baked, or as gold and silver glowing in a furnace."[14] "The blood of the martyrs is the

---

[13] Ignatius of Antioch, *Letter to the Romans*, chap. 4.

[14] *The Martyrdom of Polycarp*, chap. 15.

seed of the Church," Tertullian tells us in his *Apology*.[15] It is the seed of the Church because, by following Christ unto death, the saints and martyrs were able to place present life in perspective and place their hope in the life to come, a life in which they believed they would see God face-to-face.

Jesus told his disciples that he no longer called them servants but friends (Jn 15:15). According to Thomas Aquinas, "charity is the friendship of man for God."[16] The early saints and martyrs were true friends of God, for they clearly displayed the three marks of friendship elucidated in the tradition of classical Greece and embraced by the Church's theological tradition in such thinkers as St. Augustine and Thomas Aquinas. To begin with, their relationship with the Lord was rooted in benevolence, whereby a person actively seeks the well-being of her or her

---

[15] Tertullian, *Apology*, 50.13.

[16] Thomas Aquinas, *Summa theologiae*, II-II, q. 23, a. 1, resp.

friend. It was also reciprocal in that the relationship was mutual and freely accepted and entered into by each of the persons involved. Finally, it brought about a sense of mutual indwelling, whereby each person carried the other in his or her heart, resulting in a sense of being, as Aristotle would say, "a single soul dwelling in two bodies."[17] The point here is that authentic friendship brings about a union of minds and hearts that enables each party to know, almost intuitively, the thought and desires of the other by means of a connatural union of mind and heart. Being a saint or "friend of God" is another way of speaking about holiness, the most important attribute necessary for anyone seeking to find God in all things.

---

[17] This saying is attributed to Aristotle by Diogenes Laertius. For the marks of friendship see Paul J. Wadell, *Friendship and the Moral Life* (Notre Dame, IN: University of Notre Dame Press, 1989), 130-41.

Conclusion

Although we can make positive statements about God, we also sense that his mysterious and infinite nature far exceeds the capacity of our finite human minds to comprehend him fully. He conceals even as he reveals. He is present in creation by virtue of his power to keep all things in being, the vestiges of himself that he has imprinted in the created order, and in the image of himself in which he created us. He is also hidden, however, in a way that defies explanation, and which can best be understood by embracing the apophatic way of unknowing. What we know about God, in other words, must be offset by what we can say who or what God is not.

We should not be surprised by any of this. After all, are we not, at one and the same time, both present to yet hidden from one another? Do we ever really get to know anyone fully? Do we even know our closest most intimate friends fully? Do we ever really come to understand ourselves fully? If not, how can we ever possibly expect it of God? There will always be a certain amount of mystery in our relationship with ourselves and others, and there will always remain a certain amount of mystery in our relationship with God. Even the saints, the veritable "friends of God," those who gave witness to their Lord and Master and who gave themselves to him to the point of dying for him, did not understand everything about him.

There is a mysterious, unknowable quality in our Triune God of Love that defies conceptual expression. The best we can hope for is a union of wills that brings about a certain intuitive knowledge that friends share with one another. Such a relationship is rooted in trust and affirms that the complementary ways of positive and negative theology, of the cataphatic and apophatic ways converge in the way of the Gospel, the way of Love, the way of the Lord Jesus. If we walk the way of holiness and become friends of God, we will discover Jesus in our midst and God's presence in all things, in all people, in all times, places, and circumstances. Because of his hidden presence, however, both within us, around us, and among us, we will find that his presence in the New Creation is never static but constantly changing and taking shape. His presence, we might say, is a revealing dynamic hiddenness, one that bids us to discover him ever anew in the simple, ordinary things in the adventure of life that ultimately brings us face-to-face with the infinite mystery of that which lies beyond the thin veil of death that separates us from the world to come.

Led by the Spirit

Have you ever found yourself yearning for the God whose Spirit you believe is already dwelling within you? If so, what does such yearning mean? How can God be, at one and the same time, both present and absent? Why does he conceal himself as he reveals? Why does he reveal himself as he conceals? Why is he such an elusive God? How can Jesus be both within us and in our midst? Will you ever be able to know God as he truly is? Will you ever be able to exhaust his infinite mystery? Why has God chosen to reveal himself to you? What have you revealed to God about yourself? What are you hiding from him? Is your yearning for him actually an intimate sharing in his Spirit? Does God yearn for you as you yearn for him?

Prayer to the Holy Spirit

Come, Holy Spirit. Help me to sense your presence in my deep inner yearnings. Help me to yearn with your yearning, to groan with your groaning. Help me to understand God's hidden presence in my life and to listen to the still small voice comforting voice of your merciful love. Fill me with your love.

Help me to reveal to you what I have kept hidden from you for so long. Release me from the shame that makes me run away and hide from you. Give me a deep awareness of your love for me and your desire to transform me from within. Come, Holy Spirit, come. Mary, my mother, woman filled with the grace of the Spirit, pray for me.

Chapter Three

Walking by Faith

Thus far, we have determined that Jesus, the New Adam, came into the world to heal humanity and the whole created world of its wounds and to elevate them to new heights. The New Creation, which he inaugurated through the mysteries of the Incarnation and his passion, death, and resurrection, is quietly taking shape and will eventually reach its full stature as God's providential plan unfolds. Jesus, the Lord of history, is at work in the world through the presence and influence of his Spirit, who imbues the Church, his Mystical Body, with the power to change the hearts of men and redirect them in ways that abide by the new commandment he gave to his disciples: "I give you a new commandment, that you love one another. Just as I have

loved you, you also should love one another"
(Jn 13:34).

If Jesus' presence in the world is real and
not a mere subjective experience on the part
of believers, then we must ask ourselves how
we can perceive his presence in the world
around us. What interpretive tools can we use
to verify the presence of his Spirit, who is
quietly shaping the present historical reality
into the New Creation envisioned by God
from before the dawn of time? How do we
sense the existence of his kingdom in our
hearts and in our midst? Jesus himself, who
spoke in parables and used metaphors from
nature and everyday life to convey to us a
sense of the inbreaking of God's kingdom,
gives us a hint about the how we must approach such questions. For instance, he likes
using the example of the mustard seed to
remind us how God works in our midst and
how his kingdom can be seen only when
viewed through the eyes of faith. In one
parable, for example, he reminds us that the

kingdom of God grows at its own pace and will come to fulfillment in due time (Mk 4:30-32). Elsewhere, he states that we would be able to move mountains and uproot trees if we had faith the size of a mustard seed (Mt 17:20; Lk 17:6). From such images, we learn that, like the mustard seed, God's kingdom grows at its own rate, according to its own internal rhythm. It welcomes and encourages our human cooperation but is not tied to it. What is more, even a small modicum of faith will enable us to work wonders beyond our wildest dreams. It is only by viewing the world around us through the eyes of faith, even if it be as small as the mustard seed, that we can move the scales from our eyes that blind us from seeing things as they really are. The real mountains moved by faith are our own prejudices and biases that prevent us from seeing the gentle movement of the Spirit in our midst.

The Light of Faith

The metaphor of sight is another way in which we can see the importance of faith for sensing the presence of the Spirit and the in-breaking of the kingdom in our midst. Light is necessary for us to see the world around us. Although we have an inborn capacity to see, without light we would be condemned to living in a world of darkness. Light is the medium by which our eyes receive data from the external world so that our brains can, upon receiving the information, transform it into the images that enable us to see the things around us so we can make our way in life.

Common sense tells us that there is a correspondence between the objective order and what our eyes tells us is there. At the same time, we understand that our eyes are capable of receiving only a portion of the myriad kinds of waves that permeate the atmosphere. For instance, we are unable to see infrared light, radio waves, x-rays, and many other forms of energy that permeate the air around us. When people take their glasses off, they usually have a blurry vision of the world around them. Because of damage to or a lack of certain visual receptors in their eyes, the color blind are limited in what they can see. Animals experience the world around them in very different ways because of their different visual capacities. The point being made here is that there is much more to the objective order than meets the eye. When it comes to Christianity, the New Creation inaugurated by Jesus' Incarnation and paschal mystery can only be seen through the eyes of faith.

"Faith," we are told in the Letter to the Hebrews, "is the assurance of things hoped for, the conviction of things not seen" (Heb 11:1). It is a gift from God, a treasure that, through the influence of grace (the supernatural parallel to what light is in the natural order), enables us to have firm convictions about things we cannot see. If grace perfects nature, then the light of grace perfects the natural light of human reason and enables us to experience the world around us with the eyes of faith. Faith enlightens the mind, strengthens the will, and tames the passions. It changes our focus in life, engendering hope which, in turn, gives rise to love. Our journey through life is meant to be a walk by faith. We make our way to God and the beatific vision (heaven) only by walking in the light of his grace. Because we believe God exists and has called us to himself, we set out on our journey of faith and hope one day to arrive there. We must do so, however, one step at a time, seeking to follow the way of the Lord Jesus, "the pioneer and perfecter of our faith" (Heb 12:2), by loving one another as he has loved us (Jn 13:34).

Interpreting the Books of Life

When we view life through the eyes of faith, we interpret what we see there by putting on the mind of Jesus and clothing ourselves in his spiritual outlook. In time, we find ourselves viewing everything against the backdrop of God's loving, providential care since it is no longer we who live, but Christ who is living in us. This new spiritual outlook extends to all areas of life that touch us in meaningful ways in our daily existence.

There are four such areas (or books) of life, each of which covers a different horizon of our spiritual journey: the books of creation, God's Word, our interior life, and the Book of Life itself. "Some people," St. Augustine tells us, "read books in order to find God. Yet there is a great book, the very appearance of created things." God has planted vestiges of himself in the world around us. When we discover them, the whole of the created order cries out, "God made me!"[18] The same holds true for the

---

[18] Augustine of Hippo, *Sermon Mai.* 126.6. Cited in Vernon J. Bourke, ed., *The Essential Augustine* (Indianapolis, IN: Hackett, 1974), 123.

Word of God itself as revealed in Sacred Scripture. Augustine himself tells us: "For now treat the Scripture of God as the face of God. Melt in its presence."[19] As far as our own personal lives are concerned, Jesus himself said that the kingdom of God was within us and among us (Lk 17:21).[20] When we ponder the movements within our hearts and in our relationships with others, we can discern signs of the Lord's calling us to deeper intimacy with him, ourselves, and those around us. Finally, the Book of Life, referred to six times in the Book of Revelation (Rev. 3:5, 13:8, 17:8, 20:12, 20:15, 21:27), stands for the end time when history will draw to a close and everyone must give an account of their

---

[19] Augustine of Hippo, *Sermon* 22.7. Cited in Robert Louis Wilken, *The Spirit of Early Christian Thought* (New Haven: Yale University Press, 2003), 50.

[20] See *The Catholic Study Bible*, New American Bible Revised Edition, 2d ed. (Oxford: Oxford University, 2011), note to Lk 17:21.

lives before God. Those whose names are recorded there will live forever in the presence of God. Their reward for their faith in Christ and their lives of holiness is life everlasting as part of the communion of saints in heaven.

These four books—Creation, Scripture, the human person, and the last things—share much in common with the four senses of Scripture developed during the patristic era: the literal, allegorical, tropological (moral), and anagogical.[21] The literal sense refers to the surface meaning of the text and would be understood today as the historical meaning of the text as revealed through the historical critical method. The allegorical meaning is a spiritual sense that shows what a given text tells us about Christ and his body, the Church. The tropological (or moral) sense tells us something about our human makeup

---

[21] See Henri de Lubac, *Exégèse médiévale: les quatre sens de l'écriture*, vol. 2 (Aubier: Editions Montaigne, 1956), 643-56.

(especially the soul) and how we should live from day to day. Finally, the anagogical sense tells us something about the end times and what we are to expect when history draws to a close and the consummation of time itself. In the thirteenth century, Augustine of Denmark summarized these four senses as follows: "The literal teaches historical events; the allegorical, what to believe; the moral, how to act; the anagogical, what to hope for."[22] Although somewhat overshadowed by the prevalent use of the historical critical method in interpreting God's Word, these four senses continue to this day to influence the Catholic understanding of how the face of

---

[22] "*Littera gesta docet, quid credas allegoria, moralis quid agas, quid speras anagogia.*" See The Pontifical Biblical Commission, *The Interpretation of the Bible in the Church* (Vatican City: Liberia Editrice Vaticana, 1993), 78.

God speaks us in the Scriptures and else-where.[23]

More an attitude of spiritual understanding than a method of determined terms, these spiritual senses can be found outside of Scripture: in the Book of Nature, the movement of history, in Christian and pagan poetry, and in that veritable summit of earthly existence, the Liturgy. In a very general way, they also correspond to the above-mentioned books in this way: the literal sense (the book of Creation), the allegorical sense (the book of God's Word), the tropological (moral) sense (the book of the human person), and the anagogical sense (the Book of Life itself). The spiritual senses should not be thought of as an imposition by the reader of patterns extrinsic to the text (what modern exegetes would refer to as "eisegesis"), but the revelation of immanent designs, some of which exist visibly in

---

[23] The Pontifical Biblical Commission, *The Interpretation of the Bible in the Church*, 77-84.

the text and others of which are found beneath the words themselves are accessible only to the mind through the eyes of faith. These books and spiritual senses help us to crack open the external grind of the text, delve beneath the appearances of things, and get to the real spiritual fruit that nourishes our hearts and gives us life.

Encountering the Stranger

If all of this sounds a bit too abstract, it may help if we employ this approach to how we encounter a stranger or someone hardly unknown to us. When we meet such a person (let's call her "Mary"), it would do well for us, first of all, to ponder her place in the book of Creation. Even though we do not know much about her, the eyes of faith tell us that she has been created in the image of God, has been in his mind from all eternity, and lives and moves and has her being in him. God created her, is creating her, and continues to keep her in existence from one moment to the next. It is also important to remember that she is a part of God's New Creation and that, even if she is unaware or does not yet completely accept it, her fallen nature has been redeemed, is being redeemed, and will be redeemed by the blood of Christ through his death on the cross. What is more, when you look upon her, remember that the Holy Spirit is at work in her life and wishes to lead her along the way of holiness so that one day she will see God face-to-face.

In addition to the book of Creation, let us also ponder Mary's significance in the light of God's revealed Word, especially with regard to Christ and the Church. Scripture tells us that we are members of his body (1 Cor 12:12). Jesus is seeking to befriend Mary and is constantly calling her to take off the old self, put on the new, so that she might share in his glorified existence (Eph 4:22-24; Col 3:1-17). What is more, he wishes her to share in the corporate consciousness of the new humanity that, as the New Adam, he has regained for us by virtue of his paschal mystery. Through the eyes of faith, we see that Mary is not a stranger at all, but a friend or, at the very least, a potential friend (Jn 15:15). It would also do well for us to inquire about the specifics of Mary's life. We should try to get to know her by asking her about those things in her life that make her a unique part of God's providential plan: her family, friends, and loved ones, her status in life, her profession, and her interests. Every person we meet is unique in all the world and a valued part of God's plan. The more we understand and appreciate this, the more we will come to cherish every person we meet as a child of God and therefore as a brother or sister in the Lord.

By pondering the specifics of Mary's life, we are led into viewing her unique human existence and its significance for our own spiritual lives. The tropological (moral) sense reminds us that Mary is more than just her material, physical appearance; she is also a spiritual being with a soul that, however tarnished or disfigured, has the capacity to reflect the beauty of God's love to others. Because we share in the corporate conscious-ness of Jesus, the New Adam, Mary also tells us much about ourselves. When we look upon her, we can see a reflection of our own lives. Her various strengths and weaknesses urge us to ponder our own limitations and lead us to a deeper commitment to open our hearts to the movement of the Spirit in our lives so that God's grace can work its trans-forming wonders within our hearts. Mary is unique but also similar, different from us yet also very much alike. Her walk on the way of holiness should encourage us to do the same. Her departure from that path, as can happen, should lead us to meet her where she is and encourage her to find her way back. Her story is a part of our story. We should never take her (or anyone) for granted.

Finally, we can look upon Mary in light of the last things. We see in her someone whose name should be written in the Book of Life. We see in her someone who lives in hope and anticipates its fulfillment. Like us, she is a restless pilgrim, making her way to her final destination, to her resting place in God's loving and intimate embrace. We see in her someone who, like us, must one day face the four last things of death, judgment, heaven, and hell. As we ponder her, we hope that our compassionate and merciful God will look kindly upon her and draw her to his side when she leaves this earth and is ready to meet him face-to-face. The anagogical meaning of Mary's life reminds us that there is more to life than what meets the eye. We see her as someone who, like us, is a fallen creature redeemed by the blood of our Lord and Savior, Jesus Christ. We see ourselves in her, as we hope she will see herself in us. We do this because we look upon her through the eyes of faith, see in her the person God intended her to be from all eternity, and believe in our hearts that God will not abandon her to her own devices. We look upon her with gratitude to a God who loves us despite our faults and failings and who, because of his infinite and boundless nature, looks upon her as the apple of her eye and the only person in existence. We also see in her someone who, like us, is on a journey that will never end because our God is a God of infinite mystery and is always disclosing something more to discover about him. What is more, it is the Spirit who leads us on this journey, the Spirit of Christ, the Advocate, the Paraclete, the Comforter. We need only look for and respond to his quiet and ever-subtle promptings.

Led by the Spirit

Jesus told his disciples that he would be with them even to the end of time (Mt 28:20). To be led by the Spirit means that we are committed first to a life of prayer. Prayer is the space in our lives that we turn over to God. We can do this in many ways: through petitions, meditation, the reading of Scripture, contemplation—to name a few. Since we are both individual and social by nature, it follows that our prayer must preserve a delicate balance in our lives between personal devotion and membership to Christ's body, the Church.

Prayer is the air we breathe that helps us to live a life in the Spirit. If we are not aware of the Spirit's presence in our lives, it may very well be because we have not spent enough time in our lives seeking the Lord in prayer. Any close relationship needs to be nurtured by time spent in the presence of the other. The same is true of our rapport with God. We nurture our relationship with him when we seek him in prayer with body, mind, and spirit. If we do not pray, we can never be on intimate terms with God. If we do not pray, we will not understand what it means to live a life led by the Spirit. If we do not pray, we may know about the gifts, but we will never know what it means to possess them and to use them. For this reason, we need to ask ourselves some very important questions. How do we pray? How do we respond to the promptings of the Spirit in our lives? How do the gifts manifest themselves in our judgments, decisions, and actions? These and other questions should help us to recognize God as our deepest need and to see prayer as the means to filling it.

To draw close to God in prayer means we are responding to the movement of grace in our lives and are open to the promptings of the Spirit. The gifts represent those specific helps God gives us to follow his will more closely in the daily circumstances of our lives. *Wisdom* enables us to make sound judgments about the things of God. *Understanding* helps us to grasp more fully what we believe. *Knowledge* does the same regarding the things of the earth. *Counsel* helps us discern the right course of action. *Fortitude* gives us confidence in the Lord in the midst of adversity. *Piety* fills us with a sense of reverence for God. *Fear of the Lord* gives us a sense of dread at the possibility of offending Him. Taken together, the gifts assure the believer of God's concrete presence and action in the face of every possible challenge. They are the winds that blow the sails of our souls and enable us to navigate our way through the difficult waters of life. Without them, none of us would make much headway in the spiritual life.

When talking about their presence in the life of believers, we should think of the gifts as working in harmony and as having a synergetic effect on us. "The whole is greater than the sum of the parts," we might say. They operate in concert with one another and rarely in isolation. They do not bring notice to themselves or even to the person upon whom they are bestowed. Their purpose is to give glory to God by transforming us ever more closely into his image and likeness. That is not to say they are always in use. In any given circumstance, the Spirit activates them as the need arises. The direction process helps us to nurture our relationship with God through prayer and be open to the promptings of the Spirit in our lives. When all is said and done, it all comes down to our co-operating with God's free offer of grace, of which there is always abundance.

Conclusion

Viewing the world around us through the eyes of faith enables us to think, speak, and act as Jesus did. This great gift is the means by which the other theological virtues of hope and love take root in our minds and hearts. It is also the way the Holy Spirit enters our souls and showers us with his manifold gifts and fruits. In the end, it is the Spirit who leads us in our journey through life and helps us interpret the four books of Creation, God's

Word, our interior life, and the last things. These insights enable us to stay in touch with the Spirit because they encourage us to lift our hearts and minds to God and lay before him our innermost needs and petitions.

In the end, it is the Spirit's fruits of "love, joy, peace, patience, kindness, generosity, faithfulness, gentleness, and self-control" (Gal 5:22) that help us sense the presence of the Lord in our hearts and in our midst. The Evil One sows the seeds of confusion and discord wherever he goes. Spirit, by way of contrast, brings a deep sense of inner peace about the decisions we make, the actions we take, and the people who accompany us on our journey. As the Apostle Paul states, "...the peace of God, which surpasses all understanding, will guard your hearts and minds in Christ Jesus" (Phil 4:7). Jesus extends to us the peace of his Spirit, a peace the world cannot give. The presence of his Spirit in our lives, in other words, affirms Jesus' promise that he would not leave us to ourselves but be always with us, even until the end of time.

How do we sense the presence of the Lord in our hearts and in our midst? The answer to this question has changed little in the centuries since Jesus breathed his Spirit upon his disciples and ascended to the right hand of the Father. We do so by turning to him in prayer, receiving the Church's sacraments, trying our best to love as he loved, and allowing his Spirit to dwell within us. Living in the Spirit is another way of speaking about the way of holiness. "The wind blows where it chooses," we are told in the Gospel of John (Jn 3:8). The same can be said for the movement of the Spirit in our lives. If we stay close to him, we can be sure that we will be led along the right path and sense the Lord's presence even in the most unexpected of places.

Led by the Spirit

Do you look at Life through the eyes of faith or doubt, a hermeneutics of trust or suspicion? In what ways does faith enlighten reason? Does reason give anything to faith? Are the two ever opposed to one another? How do they complement each other? How would you describe the relationship between the two? How do they help us interpret the books of creation, God's Word, the spiritual life, and the last things? How do they help us find Jesus in the people we encounter? How do they help us follow the promptings of the Spirit? Why is prayer so important for the life of faith? Why is it so important for our spiritual journey? Can we find our way to God without it? How does it help us sense and follow the Spirit's lead?

Prayer to the Holy Spirit

Come, Holy Spirit. Deepen my faith and trust in your loving presence. Help me to let go and to walk by faith. Help me to interpret the events of the day through the eyes of trust rather than suspicion. Help me to be sensitive to your promptings so that I may interpret correctly the events of the day. Help me to turn to you in times of difficulty and to listen to your still small voice for the proper steps to take. Help me to sense your presence in all the people I meet and in all that happens to me. Come, Holy Spirit, come. Mary, my mother, woman filled with the grace of the Spirit, pray for me.

Chapter Four

Practicing God's Presence

It is one thing to interpret the signs of God's presence in our midst and within ourselves, and quite another to actually live in his presence from one moment to the next. God is everywhere, our Christian faith tells us. We can see him in the books of Creation, God's Word, the human person, and the Book of Life itself. We have tools that help us read these books and interpret their meaning for our lives. We do so under the guidance of the Holy Spirit, who showers us with his manifold gifts that bear fruit in our lives and lead us into the presence of God himself. The question before us now is whether all of this is a mere abstraction, a pious hope, or if we truly experience God's presence in our lives, in the day-to-day events of our earthly sojourn. How, in other words, can we practice living in the presence of God? What concrete steps can we take that will enable us to become more aware of his presence in our daily lives?

The Sacrament of the Present Moment

When speaking about living in God's presence, spiritual writers often speak of the "Practice of the Presence of God" and the "Sacrament of the Present Moment."[24] This concept brings together two very important modalities of Christian thought—sacramentality and time—each of which is intimately connected to the other and to the manner in which God interacts with his crea-

---

[24] See, for example, Brother Lawrence, *The Practice of the Presence of God*, ed. Harold J. Chadwick (Gainesville, FL: Bridge-Logos, 1999), 1-6; Jean-Pierre de Caussade, *Abandonment to Divine Providence*, trans. John Beevers (Garden City, NY: Image Books, 1966), 23-24.

tion. According to the *Catechism of the Catholic Church*, "[s]acraments are efficacious signs of grace, instituted by Christ and entrusted to the Church, by which divine life is dispensed to us."[25] Time, by way of contrast, is one of the four dimensions that, along those of height, depth, and width, comprises the physical boundaries of world we live in.

Sacraments are the manner in which God continues to interact with us after Christ ascended to heaven and sent the Holy Spirit upon the nascent Church. They are actions Christ mediated through concrete, visible signs such as water, oil, the imposition of hands, and, of course, the bread and wine offered at Eucharist. When looked at more closely, the concept of sacramentality can be expanded in analogous fashion to embrace God's entire plan of redemption. When seen in this light, Christ can be said to be the

---

[25] *Catechism of the Catholic Church* (Vatican City: Libreria Editrice Vaticana, 1994), no. 1131.

"Sacrament of God;" the Church, the "Sacrament of Christ;" and the seven sacraments, the "Sacraments of the Church."[26] Since these "sacraments" in the wider, analogous sense of the word, reflect the actions of the Godhead, which themselves flow from the very being of God himself, we can speak of our "Sacramental God," the only qualifier being that the aspect of materiality becomes a secondary feature in the definition.[27] Even this, however, takes on new significance when we realize that part of God's salvific place was to have his Son enter our world so that he could recapitulate all things in himself, have them share in his divinity and, in effect, become "divinized."

---

[26] For these and other analogous uses of the term "sacrament." See Michael Schmaus, *Dogma*, vol. 5, *The Church as Sacrament* (London: Sheed and Ward, 1975), 1-9.

[27] See Dennis J. Billy, *Evangelical Kernels: A Theological Spirituality of the Religious Life* (Staten Island, NY: Alba House, 1993), 126-27.

Our Christian faith affirms that time is not eternal but a creation of God himself; otherwise, it could make a claim of divinity for itself. Like the rest of Creation, it has a beginning and an end: it came into being and will one day cease to exist. The Christian doctrines regarding the last things—death, judgement, heaven, and hell—remind us that the movement of history is drawing to a close and that Christ himself will bring it to its consummation. Its end, however, is not a disappearance, but a transformation. As death is not the end of life but a threshold to a new form of existence, time itself will be transformed into a fuller, deeper reality: like wine from grape, time itself is destined to take on a different shape.[28] Chronological or measured time (*Chronos*) will become sacred time (*Kairos*), which brushes up against the threshold of eternity. Human beings have the

---

[28] See Dennis Billy, "Biding Time," in *As There as the Sky* (Wipf and Stock, 2018), 22.

unique position in all of God's creation to be able to experience both. We have two feet on the ground as we walk through this earthly life, yet we look up at the stars at night and stand in awe at the beauty of God's creation. We are citizens of two cities: the City of God and the City of Man, with the latter finally being transformed and taken up into the latter.

When time and sacramentality converge in the notion of the "Sacrament of the Present Moment," we find, at one and the same time, both a longing for God and a thirst for the transformation of time itself. While we recognize their importance in leading us to God, we look beyond the sacraments, beyond the Church, and beyond Christ, to the Triune God himself, whose providential will is quietly working in our hearts through these visible sacramental signs of his love to ultimately draw us to himself. Similarly, although we find ourselves in time, we yearn to be outside of time and recognize within ourselves a deep-down desire to experience eternity in the present moment. If Creation is *guttatim* ("drop by drop"), it follows that time itself, the created backdrop against which the rest of creation comes into being, is called into being from one moment to the next. "With the Lord one day is like a thousand years, and a thousand years as like one day" (2 Pt 3:8). When seen in this light, *Chronos,* or measured time, is a man-made interpretation of true time, while *Kairos* (sacred time), in turn, is the yearning for eternity within our hearts that reminds us of what and for whom we were made. The question arises: How can we enter into this "Sacrament of the Present Moment?" How, in other words, can we live continually in the presence of God? And why?

Why Live in the Presence of God?

Before looking into the practical ways in which we can live in God's presence from one moment to the next, we would do well to consider the reasons why we should do so in the first place. Spiritual writers such as Brother Lawrence, O.C.D., and Jean-Pierre de Caussade, S.J., have provided wonderful insights about how to practice the presence of God and what it means to surrender ourselves entirely to Divine Providence.[29] Brother Lawrence, a simple seventeenth-century Discalced Carmelite lay brother, who lived in Paris and served as his friary's cook and shoemaker, points out some of the essential conditions for attaining the presence of God. Among them he lists: purity of life, faithfulness, looking to God before beginning any task, patience, not being upset over one's failures, and perseverance.[30] "The practice of the presence of God," he states, "is somewhat hard in the beginning, yet pursued faithfully it imperceptibly works most mar-

---

[29] See n. 24 above.

[30] Brother Lawrence, *The Practice of the Presence of God*, 115-17.

velous effects within the soul."[31] Similarly, Jean-Pierre de Caussade, an eighteenth-century French Jesuit, highlights the importance of following God's will wherever it may lead. What is more, he claims that there is no secret method for doing this: "Surely we must realize that in every age, including this one, God's will works through every moment, making each one holy and giving it a supernatural quality. Can we imagine that in the days of old there was a secret method of abandoning oneself to the divine will that is now out of date? And had the saints of those early times any other secret apart from that of obeying God's will from moment to moment? And will not God continue until the end of the world to pour out his grace upon all the souls who utterly abandon themselves to him?"[32]

---

[31] Ibid., 116.

[32] Caussade, *Abandonment to Divine Providence*, 50.

In his work, *Conformity to the Will of God*, Alphonsus de Liguori, the eighteenth-century giant in moral and spiritual matters, whom Pope St. John Paul II referred to as the Augustine of the modern era, points out that doing God's will involves a movement from servile fear of God (childlike obedience), to a sense of duty and respect (conformity to God's will) and, ultimately, to a deep love (uniformity with God's will).[33] The latter, he maintains, is the goal we all should be moving toward. We do God's will out of love for him, and because our wills are so closely united to his that we cannot even distinguish the difference between his will and our own. Such was the meaning of Jesus' words when he said, "The Father and I are one" (Jn 10:30).

---

[33] Alphonsus de Liguori, *Conformity to the Will of God* in *The Way of Salvation and Perfection*, The Complete Works of St. Alphonsus de Liguori, ed. Eugene Grimm, vol. 2 (Brooklyn: Redemptorist Fathers, 1926), 353-90.

Elsewhere, in his treatise *The Presence of God*, Alphonsus highlights three reasons why we should practice living in the presence of God. The first effect produced by this holy exercise is the avoidance of sin. In his mind, "…there is no more efficacious means of subduing the passions, resisting temptations, and consequently of avoiding sin, than the remembrance of God's presence."[34] We sin because we lose sight of God's presence and mistakenly think that what we do in darkness will never be brought to light. The second effect is the practice of virtue. We would seek to do all things well, he states, if we were constantly aware that God was looking at all our actions. We would grow in virtue out of our desire to please God in all things.[35] The third effect of this holy practice is union with God. According to Alphonsus, "…it is an

---

[34] Alphonsus de Liguori, *The Presence of God* in *Talking with God*, 1 in *Four Treatises on the Interior Life from St. Alphonsus Liguori*, 111.

[35] Ibid., 115.

infallible rule that love is always increased by the presence of the object loved."[36] The more we are aware of God's presence in our lives, the more we will strive to be like him and love as he loves. These three effects—the avoidance of sin, the practice of virtue, and union with God—correspond the purgative, illuminative, and unitive dimensions of our spiritual journey. Practicing the presence of God, in other words, is the foundation of an authentic spiritual life a sure way to growth in holiness.[37]

Practicing the Presence of God

According to Alphonsus, the practice of the presence of God is a function of the two major powers of the soul: intellect and will. "This exercise," he states, "consists partly in the operation of the understanding, and part-

---

[36] Ibid., 116.
[37] Ibid., 111.

ly in the operation of the will: of the under-standing—in beholding God present; of the will—in uniting the soul to God, by acts of humiliation, of adoration, of love, and the like."[38] These faculties set us apart from the rest of Creation and enable us to perceive and desire things beneath appearances and beyond what meets the eye.

We can practice the presence of God through our intellect in four ways: through the imagination, through the eyes of faith, by seeing him in creation, and by looking within.[39] The first method involves simply imagining that he is in our company wherever we may be. We can use various scenes from the Gospels (Jesus lying in a manger, his flight into Egypt, his hidden life in Nazareth, his miracles, his passion, his death on the cross, his resurrection) to feed our imagination so that can see him in our minds and sense his

---

[38] Ibid., 118.
[39] Ibid., 118-28.

presence. While this approach can be very beneficial, care must be taken to not give way to illusion or mistake it for Jesus' real presence in the Eucharist. The second method is more secure and "consists in beholding with eyes of faith God present with us in every place, in considering that he encompasses us, that he sees and observes whatever we do."[40] It is more secure because it does not tire the mind and can enliven our faith when we make affectionate acts of the will such as, "My God, I believe firmly that You are here present."[41] The third method is "to recognize him [God] in his creatures, which have from him their being, and their power of serving us."[42] According to Alphonsus, "God is in the water to wash us, in the fire to warm us, in the sun to enlighten us, in the food to nourish us, in clothes to cover us, and in like manner in all other things that he has created for our

---

[40] Ibid., 119-20.

[41] Ibid., 120.

[42] Ibid., 121.

use."[43] Seeing God in all created things inspires acts of love and gratitude for all that he has given us. The fourth way and most perfect way of practicing the presence of God is to consider his presence within us. For Alphonsus, "[i]t is necessary to know that God is present in us, in a manner different from that in which he is present in other creatures; in us he is present as in his own temple and his own house."[44] God wishes to make his abode in our hearts, making them tabernacles of his loving presence. By looking within, we become aware of God's love for us and are capable of appreciating his presence all around us.

We can practice the presence of God through the will in three ways: by frequently raising our hearts to God, by making specific intentions to please God, and by recollecting ourselves with God. The best way to imple-

---

[43] Ibid.

[44] Ibid., 123.

ment the first approach is by making short, fervent loving affections to God. Brief but potent prayers such as "My God, I wish only you and nothing else!" or "I give myself entirely to you!" and "I love you more than myself!"[45] can be done at any time or place. Such prayers are particularly helpful in the morning when we awake, when they are said before any longer vocal or mental prayers, and especially in time of temptation. The second way of preserving the presence of God through the will "is to renew always in distracting employments the intention of performing them all with the intention of pleasing God."[46] Whenever we are distracted (as often happens), we can refocus our hearts on the reason behind our actions by simply saying, "My God, may all be for your glory"[47] It is also helpful to use certain times (e.g., whenever the clock strikes) or signs (e.g.,

---

[45] Ibid., 129-30.

[46] Ibid., 132.

[47] Ibid.

whenever we enter our room or look at the crucifix) as a way of developing the habit of continual recourse to God.[48] The third and final way of practicing the presence of God through the will is to take some time out whenever we find ourselves distracted and go to our room or to the chapel in order to re-collect ourselves in the presence of God.[49] Sometimes, it is necessary to get away from the busyness of life and get back in touch with ourselves by simply letting go of everything and placing ourselves in the presence of God. Doing so will help us gather our resources and focus them on the one thing that really matters.

The practice of the presence of God is a spiritual exercise that focuses our minds and hearts on God in a way that strengthens our resolve to do all things for the love of God because of God's love for us. The more we

---

[48] Ibid.

[49] Ibid., 133-34.

practice it, the more aware will we be of God's presence in our lives and the more intent will we be to do all things for the glory of God. The constant use of this spiritual exercise will purify our hearts, guide along the way of virtue, and foster fellowship and communion with God. It forms the foundation of the spiritual life and what it means to be a disciple of Christ and child of the Father.

Conclusion

The practice of the presence of God enables us to live in the present moment and is a sure and reliable way to growth in holiness. This holy exercise helps us to avoid sin, grow in virtue, and gradually find our way to God. It also goes hand-in-hand with the threefold way of purgation, illumination, and union that forms the existential backdrop of every spiritual journey. This movement away from sin to the practice of virtue and ultimate union with God takes shape in each of us at different rates and tends to be more cyclical than linear. That is to say that during our lives on earth we will likely experience many moments of cleansing, growth, and communion. Our rate of growth, moreover, is commensurate with how we cooperate with God's grace and respond to the movement of the Spirit in our lives.

Another way of saying this is that the more we become aware of the presence of God in our lives, the more will we recognize that grace everywhere abounds and is always there for the asking. We practice the presence of God with our minds through the imagination, with the eyes of faith, by pondering God's creation, and by looking within our own hearts. We can also practice it with our wills by making short, heartfelt prayers to God, periodically renewing our intentions to follow God's will, and stepping away, at times, from life's hectic pace to recollect ourselves and make sure our priorities are in the right place. The details of the practice are clear. Whether we actually do carry them by cooperating with the movement of God's grace in our lives remains to be seen.

We can practice the presence of God only because he himself wishes to be present to us and has given us the grace to do so. He created time and space for us to dwell in and flourish so that he himself could dwell and flourish in the interior landscape of our souls. Of all the places he could possibly choose, God has eyed the human heart from all eternity as his preferred dwelling place. He sent his only Son to befriend us and make this happen. As the sacrament of God, Jesus makes God present to us in a very concrete and visible way. By practicing the presence of God, we ourselves reciprocate his love by opening our hearts to him and allowing him to live in our hearts. The spiritual journey is all about developing a growing awareness of God's presence in our lives so that we ourselves can be present in the lives of those we serve. This journey will never end because

God's love is boundless, ever merciful, and without end.

Led by the Spirit

What is the sacrament of the present moment? Why is it important? Why is it called a sacrament? How does one receive it? How does it differ from the sacraments of the Church? Have you ever felt as though you were living in the present moment? If so, how did it happen? Did you lose track of time? Where you there for a long time? Were you aware it was happening? What is it like to live in the presence of God? Have you ever tried to do so through the intellect by way of the imagination, the eyes of faith, God's creation, or looking within? Have you ever tried to do so through the will by raising your heart to God, making specific intentions to please God, or by recollecting yourself with God? Why is it important to live in the presence of God?

Prayer to the Holy Spirit

Come, Holy Spirit. Help me to live in the present moment. Let me never forget that you are always with me and that you wish to dwell within my heart at all times. Help to trust in your abiding presence in times of consolation and in times of desolation. Help me to seek your presence in my imagination, through the eyes of faith, in the beauty of creation, and by looking within my own heart. Help me to constantly turn to you with deep, heartfelt prayers. Enable me to do everything with the intention to please you. Help me to find you in the solitude of my own heart. Come, Holy Spirit, come. Mary, my mother, woman filled with the grace of the Spirit, pray for me.

Chapter Five

All the Way to Heaven

The spiritual journey has often been described as finding our way to God. Many works from the various Christian traditions have emphasized our search for God and the progress we make by means of carefully delineated spiritual exercises. Teresa of Avila's *Interior Castle* in the Catholic tradition, the anonymous *The Way of the Pilgrim* in the Orthodox tradition, and Paul Bunyan's *The Pilgrim's Progress* in the Protestant tradition all presuppose the notion of the spiritual quest for wholeness and union with God. For many such works, the notion of the threefold way of purgation, illumination, and union is the spiritual backdrop against which many such narratives unfold. Augustine's *Confes-*

sions and Thérèse of Lisieux's *The Journey of a Soul* are other examples of how two very different individuals employ the themes of the threefold way to their quest for God in the particular circumstances of their lives. Augustine's journey represents an intellectual conversion from Manichaeism to Neoplatonism, to Christianity, while the Little Flower's spiritual journey is one of simple trust in God, complete abandonment to God's will, and the experience spiritual childhood.

As profound as these and many other accounts of the spiritual journey are, they all hinge on another very important truth that is sometimes overlooked by the casual reader: our search for God presupposes the prior initiative of God's search for us; we can find our way to God only because God has first found his way to us. The mystery of the Incarnation, Jesus' death on the cross, his descent into hell, his resurrection and ascension into heaven, and his subsequent sending of the

Holy Spirit are all prerequisite stages of his ultimate goal of dwelling within our hearts. Francis Thomson's poem, *The Hound of Heaven*, is a wonderful description of God's search for us, despite our stubborn resistance to his abundant grace. He never gives up on us, even when, for all practical appearances, it looks as though we have given up on him and decided to go our own way. We find ourselves in God only because he himself long before has set out to find himself in us by luring us into relationship with him, befriending us, and living within our hearts.

Merton on the True and False Self

Thomas Merton describes our spiritual journey in terms of a movement away from the false self to the discovery of one's true self in God.[50] Holiness, he claims, is a matter of

---

[50] Thomas Merton, *New Seeds of Contemplation* (New York: New Directions, 1961), 31-32.

being our true selves. Unfortunately, we enter this world with an illusory, false self that inhibits us from becoming the persons we were truly meant to be: "I came into existence under a sign of contradiction, being someone that I was never intended to be and therefore a denial of what I am supposed to be. And thus I came into existence and non-existence at the same time because from the very start I was something that I was not."[51] We sin whenever we embrace this false self and live out of the illusions and falsehoods it presents to us about the meaning of life and about living life to the full.

Reminiscent of St. Paul's exhortation to take off the old self and put on the new (Eph 4:22-24), Merton claims that the fullness of life is all about stripping off the false self and discovering the persons whom God intends us to be. Our true identities are hidden in God, and we must journey into the mystery

---

[51] Ibid., 33-34.

of God in order to find ourselves. This is something, however, that we cannot do by ourselves: "For although I can know something of God's existence and nature of my own reason, there is no human and rational way in which I can arrive at that contact, that possession of Him, which will be the discovery of Who He really is and of Who I am in him."[52] Only God can show us the way to God. Only he can disclose to us our true identities hidden in him and bring them to light.

According to Merton, we find ourselves in God only when we allow God to find himself in us: "Our discovery of God is, in a way, God's discovery of us. We cannot go to heaven to find Him because we have no way of knowing where heaven is or what it is. He comes down from heaven and finds us."[53] Jesus entered our world to become the New Adam and, in doing so, gave us the oppor-

---

[52] Ibid., 36.
[53] Ibid., 39.

tunity to find ourselves anew in the new humanity that inhabits his New Creation. As members of his Mystical Body, we share in the collective consciousness of the New Adam and in the consciousness of God himself. Merton puts it this way: "We only know Him in so far as we are known by Him, and our contemplation of Him is a participation of His contemplation of Himself. We become contemplatives when God discovers Himself in us. At that moment, the point of our contact with Him opens out and we pass through the center of our own souls, and enter into infinite reality, where we awaken as our true self."[54] Our spiritual journey, for Merton, takes place only because God has entered our world and sought to dwell within the interior landscape of our souls. God's dwelling within us opens the way for us to dwell in God and discover our true selves.

---

[54] Ibid., 39-40.

The Two Journeys

If our finding ourselves in God is predicated on God's finding himself in us, then it is more appropriate to talk about two spiritual journeys: our journey into God and God's journey into us. While these two journeys are distinct, they are also intimately related. The former cannot take place without the latter; the latter, in turn, takes place because of God's love for creation and his desire for that love to be reciprocated. They come together, moreover, in the person of Christ who, being fully human and fully divine, sets out on both journeys and brings the rest of humanity with him on his return to the Father.

These two journeys of Christ are implied in Athanasius of Alexandria's statement, "God became man so that man might become divine."[55] Because the humanity and divinity

---

[55] See above n. 5.

of Christ are intimately related in the hypostatic union of his human and divine natures, these two journeys are themselves so closely connected that they, in effect, unite in the single journey of Christ's redemptive mission. In Christ, one cannot take place without the other. He entered our world, gave himself completely for us, to the point of dying for us, becoming our nourishment and source of hope, only so that we might reap the benefits of his Incarnation and paschal mystery and find our way to God. Christ entered our world, in other words, only so that we could accompany him back to the Father's right hand. Our true selves, our true identities, lie in our sharing in the life of God himself.

Jesus, the New Adam, freely offers us through his obedience to the Father what our first parents tried to snatch for themselves through their disobedience—a share in God's very life. Adam and Eve ate of the tree of the knowledge of good and evil because they thought that, by doing so, they would be like

God (Gn 3:5). Through their humble obedience, Jesus, the New Adam, and Mary, the New Eve, opened up the gates of paradise for us and gave us the opportunity to once again walk in fellowship with God. Because of Mary's humble and loving *fiat* and Jesus' open and willing embrace of the Father's will, our humanity is now wedded to his, and our spiritual journey is intimately linked to his return to the Father. Our spiritual journey, in other words, is deeply intertwined with his. We follow the way of the Lord Jesus because we believe that it will lead us into the presence of the Father.

A Work of the Spirit

The reason why our spiritual journey is so intimately related to his return to the Father is because Jesus has given us his Spirit to help us follow him there. The Holy Spirit is the soul of the Church and the animating force of Christ's Mystical Body. When the believing community gathers for worship, we pray to the Father "through him [Christ] and with him and in him in the unity of the Holy Spirit."[56] This unity is the life-giving principle that makes us all one in Christ. If the Holy Spirit is the bond between the Father and the Son, he is also the unifying force that integrates all believers into Christ's Mystical Body. Our return to the Father is possible only because, after his own return to the Father, Jesus sent us his Spirit to guide us and lead us home. We can find our way there only because the Spirit resides in us to show us the way.

When seen in this light, our spiritual journey is largely a work of the Holy Spirit. As we have seen, although God always acts as one, each of the three great loving actions of our Triune God is typically associated with

---

[56] *The Roman Missal*, English translation according to the third typical edition (Washington, D.C.: The United States Conference of Catholic Bishops, 2010), 633.

on the of Persons of the Trinity: Creation, with the Father, Redemption with the Son, and Sanctification with the Holy Spirit. Our spiritual journey is all about the process of our own self-discovery, of coming to know and love our truest, deepest selves. If it is true, as Merton claims, that "to be a saint means to be myself" (SC 26),[57] then the spiritual journey is all about letting go of our false selves and being open to the movement of the Spirit in our lives so that we can truly become ourselves before God and others. The Spirit, in other words, helps us to take off the old self and put on the new. By crying our "Abba, Father" (Rom 8:15) within our hearts, the Spirit reveals to us our true identities as children of God, adopted sons and daughters of the Father.

In *Abandonment to Divine Providence*, Jean-Pierre de Caussade describes the spiritual life as a movement from "us living in

---

[57] Merton, *New Seeds of Contemplation*, 31.

God" to "God living in us."[58] These two states, he claims, are very different. With the former, we occupy ourselves with all kinds of spiritual practices, such as spiritual reading, self-reflection, pious devotions, prayer, fasting, and the regular examination of our progress in the spiritual life. Everything is done by traditional disciplines as we try our best to bring our lives into conformity with Christ. Although grace is operative in this process, we still remain the principal agents in the journey. Such "living in God" follows closely the rules of the spiritual life and is a good description of what spiritual writers call the "ascetical life." We walk toward God under the influence of grace but do so in such a way that the powers of our souls remain intact and remain the primary movers in our spiritual journey.

---

[58] Caussade, *Abandonment to Divine Providence*, 59.

The latter, by way of contrast, is something altogether different. When God lives in us, we must abandon ourselves completely to the movement of the Spirit in our lives and accept everything that happens to us as coming directly from the hand of God. This is a good example of what spiritual writers call the "mystical life." In such a scenario, the Holy Spirit becomes so deeply united with us that he takes gentle possession of our souls and does so in such a way that we remain fully ourselves while responding to his promptings and discerning the Lord's will from one moment to the next. In this state of the spiritual journey, the Holy Spirit is the primary actor in our lives and calls to mind the words of the Apostle Paul, "… it is no longer I who lives, but it is Christ who lives in me" (Gal 2:20). By taking gentle possession of our souls, the Spirit incorporates us ever more deeply into the mind and heart of Christ so that it is not ourselves, but he who is living and thinking and acting in us.

Another way of understanding growth in the spiritual life as a movement from the ascetical life to the mystical life, from "living in God" to "God living in us," is to look at William of St. Thierry's *Golden Epistle*. This twelfth-century treatise on the spiritual life that describes growth in the spiritual life as a movement from the animal state (where a person is concerned with the discipline of the body) to the rational state (where the person concentrates on the discipline of the mind and the acquisition of virtue) to the spiritual state (where the person seeks to respond to the promptings of the Spirit from one moment to the next and ultimately achieves final union with God).[59] Using the tripartite Pauline anthropology of body, soul, and spirit (1Thes 5:23), William shows that some people are led by their senses, others by their rational powers, and still others by the Spirit

---

[59] William of St. Thierry, *The Golden Epistle*, nos. 41-43 (Kalamazoo, MI: Cistercian Publications, 1980), 25-26.

of God, who communes with our spirits and cries out, "Abba, Father." When the Holy Spirit communes with our own spirit in this way, that intimate union overflows into the other dimensions of our human makeup, bringing them under its gentle rule and instilling in us his manifold gifts and fruits. When seen in this light, the spiritual journey is largely about allowing the Spirit to permeate more and more every dimension of our being, so that we enter into close communion with him and are able to respond freely and spontaneously to his intimate, promptings. The ultimate goal of the spiritual life, in this respect, is to live in close communion with the Spirit of Christ so that he truly does live and move within our hearts.

All the Way to Heaven

If the kingdom of God is truly both within us and among us, it is because Jesus has given us his Spirit to accompany us on the way. St.

Catherine of Siena, the fourteenth-century Italian mystic and Doctor of the Church, is noted to have once said, "All the way to heaven is heaven, because Jesus said, 'I am the way.'"[60] When he promised his disciples that he would be with them until the end of time (Mt 28:20), Jesus meant that he would be present to them by means of his Spirit, who not only vivifies the Church and her sacraments, but through them also promises to dwell within our hearts and unite us to Christ and the other members of his body. It is the presence of the Spirit in our lives down through the ages that makes St. Catherine's words so relevant and true.

There is an interesting tension in the idea that heaven (that is, the kingdom of God) is both present to us during our spiritual journey and yet still to come. This eschatological, already-but-not-yet quality of our spiritual

---

[60] Cited in Regis Martin, *The Last Things: Death, Judgment, Heaven, Hell* (San Francisco, Ignatius Press, 1998), 39.

journey reminds us of the importance of the three theological virtues of faith, hope, and love. These virtues, as the Apostle Paul reminds us, accompany us on our journey and are, in the end, the only three things that last (1 Cor 13: 13). Faith is important because we would not even bother to set out on our spiritual journey if we did not believe that God existed, loved us, and has prepared a place for us in his kingdom. Without faith, we would be devoid of a sense of transcendence, and our journey through life would not be oriented beyond the present world. Hope, by way of contrast, accompanies us on every step of our journey by giving us a sense of anticipation of reaching our journey's end. We have a yearning for God planted within our hearts; the closer we get to our destination the deeper that yearning becomes, almost to the point that we can taste it and relish its presence even before we finally arrive. Without hope, we would get discouraged in times of difficulty and give in to the temptations of presumption (false hope) or despair (no hope). Love, the greatest of the three theological virtues, looks to the nitty gritty details of our journey to God. Every journey involves careful preparation and planning all along the way. Every step must find firm footing that will lead us to the next. The way of Jesus is the way of love. "All the way to heaven is heaven" only if we seek to follow the Lord's way by following the new commandment that he gave his disciples: "I give you a new commandment, that you love one another. Just as I have loved you, you also should love one another" (Jn 13: 34).

These three virtues are essential for our spiritual journey and gifts of God infused by the Holy Spirit in our souls. They enlighten our minds and strengthen our wills in such a way that, in time, our hearts and minds become entirely focused on the one thing that matters in life: the kingdom of God proclaimed by Jesus Christ, the Son of God, Prince of Peace, and Lord of the Universe.

Gifted in this way by the Spirit, whose proper name can itself be properly called "Gift,"[61] opens us up to receive his various gifts and fruits: the former enable us to respond spontaneously to the promptings of the Spirit in our lives, while the latter are concrete signs that the kingdom of God, while yet to come, has indeed already arrived and is present in our midst. When seen in this light, "All the way to heaven is heaven" because we have allowed God to live in us through his Spirit and lead us along the way of the Lord Jesus.

Conclusion

As we have seen, one of the primary truths of the Christian faith is that God became human so that humanity might become divine. Our spiritual journey is intimately related to Jesus' return to the Father. It is an

---

[61] See Thomas Aquinas, *Summa theologiae*, I, q. 38, a. 1, resp.

adventure, a journey into God that ultimately leads us to the discovery of our true selves. It is a movement away from the false self to the true self, a journey that takes place in our lives at different rates and speeds, depending on the how well we cooperate with the movement of the Spirit in our lives. We can take off the old self and put on the new (Eph 4:22-24) only by cooperating with the grace of God that leads us away from the self-centeredness of the old self to embrace the way of love symbolized by the way of Jesus, who laid down his life for us in order that we might live.

Jesus said, "If any want to become my followers, let them deny themselves and take up their cross and follow me" (Mk 8:34). Like Jesus, we, too, are called to lay down our lives for others; we, too, are called to enter their worlds, to give ourselves to them completely, and to become a source of nourishment and hope for them. Only in this way will we discover our true selves and walk the way of holiness. We cannot do this on our own. As we make our way through life, we must be led by the Spirit, who empowers us to follow in Jesus' footsteps by bestowing on us the virtues of faith, hope, and love, as well as his myriad of gifts and fruits.

"All the way to heaven is heaven, because Jesus said, 'I am the way.'" Jesus, the New Adam, points out the way and asks us to follow him in the Spirit. "The Spirit," as Basil of Caesarea reminds us, "is the source of holiness, a spiritual light, and he offers his own light to every mind to help it in its search for truth."[62] This spiritual light does more than merely enlighten our path for the journey. It also bonds us to the heart and mind of Christ himself and enables him to live in us and share in his consciousness. Because of Jesus, we have become members of the one redeemed humanity that is the New Adam. For most of us, this reality is still unfolding in

---

[62] Basil of Caesarea, *On the Holy Spirit*, 9.22-23. Cited in *The Liturgy of the Hours*, vol. 2(New York: Catholic Book Publishing, 1976), 975.

our lives because the eschatological, "already-but-not-yet" character of the kingdom is an integral part of our earthly journey. This journey will end when we meet God face-to-face and finally become our true selves. It will end, but it will also continue, because we will leave our false selves behind forever and spend eternity journeying into the mystery of the Triune God, whose love is infinite and without bounds.

Led by the Spirit

What has your spiritual journey been like? Has it been easy? What were some of the difficult moments? Were there times when you felt lost, perhaps even helpless? Were you been living out of your false self? Did you have a sense that your true self was crying to be let out? Where are you in your journey now? Do you have a clear sense of direction? Are you finding your way to God? Do you have a sense that Christ is accompanying you on it? Are you being led by his Spirit? Is he helping you discover your true self? Is your journey to God a reflection of his journey into your heart? How are these two journeys connected? How do they differ? Do you believe that all the way to heaven is heaven?

Prayer to the Holy Spirit

Come, Holy Spirit. Accompany me on my spiritual journey, all the way to heaven! Help me to trust in you at all times and respond to your promptings immediately, and without counting the cost. Help me to take off my false self and the new self. Help me to put on Christ so that I might become the person you desire me to become. Live in me, Dear Spirit, take possession of my soul. Shape me! Transform me! Sanctify me! Divinize me! Dwell within my heart so that I might dwell within the heart of my Lord and Savior! Come, Holy Spirit, come! Mary, my mother, woman filled with the grace of the Spirit, pray for me.

Conclusion

The way of the Lord Jesus is the way of the Spirit. This book has sought to place Life in the Spirit in the larger context of God's threefold loving actions of creation, redemption, and sanctification. It has also attempted to show how the Spirit is the soul of Christ's Mystical Body and the means by which each of its members can both share in the collective consciousness of Christ himself and sense his presence within their hearts and in their midst. It has presented openness to the Spirit as the primary means by which we walk by faith during our earthly sojourn, live in the present moment, and practice living in the presence of God from one moment to the next. Finally, it has looked to the Spirit as our primary guide in our spiritual journey, someone who lights up the path before us and who shows us where to go by means of the infused virtues of faith, hope, and charity, and especially by his many gifts and fruits.

Following Jesus means being open to and led by his Spirit. To do so, however, we must be deeply rooted in prayer and willing, through the influence of God's grace, not only to conform our hearts and minds with the Lord, but also to make them completely one ("uniform") with his. Most of all, we must be continually inviting the Spirit to enter our hearts, take up his abode there, commune with our spirits, and groan within us for the coming of the kingdom which, in a simple yet ever-elusive way, is mysteriously already in our midst. Such an invitation must come from deep within our hearts and reflect a yearning for that communion with the Father and the Son who is the Spirit himself. And so, let us pray with one heart and one voice:

> Come, Holy Spirit, fill the hearts of your faithful and enkindle in them the fire of

your love. Send forth your Spirit and they shall be created. And you shalt renew the face of the earth. Let us pray. O God, Who instructed the hearts of the faithful by the light of the Spirit, grant us in the same Spirit to be truly wise, and ever to rejoice in his consolation, through Christ, our Lord. Amen.

More Books on the Spiritual Life
By Dennis J. Billy, C.Ss.R.

Aelred of Rievaulx's Spiritual Friendship: The Classic Text and Commentary. Notre Dame, IN: Christian Classics, 2008.

Alphonsus de Liguori, Visits to the Most Holy Sacrament and to Most Holy Mary: The Classic Text Translated with a Spiritual Commentary. Notre Dame, IN: Christian Classics, 2007.

The Beauty of the Eucharist: Voices from the Church Fathers. London/Hyde Park, NY: New City Press, 2010.

Blessings of the Rosary. Liguori, MO: Liguori Publications, 2010.

The Cloud of Unknowing. Liguori, MO: Liguori Publications, 2014.

Contemplative Ethics: An Introduction. Mahwah, NJ: Paulist Press, 2011.

C. S. Lewis on the Fullness of Life: Longing for Deep Heaven. Mahwah, NJ: Paulist Press, 2009.

Encounter the Cross: Meditations on the Seven Last Words of Jesus. Liguori, MO: Liguori Publications, 2010.

Eucharist: Exploring the Diamond of Our Faith Mystic, CT: Twenty-Third Publications, 2004.

Even Today: Theology and the Inner Child. Staten Island, NY: Alba House, 1995.

Experiencing God: Fostering a Contemplative Life. Liguori, MO: Liguori Publications, 2000.

Finding Our Way to God: Spiritual Direction and the Moral Life. Liguori, MO: Liguori Publications, 2018.

Follow Him and Reclaim the World. Liguori, MO: Liguori Publications, 2016.

Going Beyond the Wound: A Spirituality for Men. Hyde Park, NY: New City Press, 2018.

Gospel Joy: Pope Francis and the New Evangelization. Hyde Park, NY: New City Press, 2014.

The Imitation of Christ: Spiritual Commentary and Reader's Guide. Notre Dame, IN: Christian Classics, 2005.

Into the Heart of Faith: Ten Steps on the Journey. Liguori, MO: Liguori Publications, 1999.

Jean-Pierre de Caussaude's Abandonment to Divine Providence: The Classic Text with a Spiritual Commentary. Notre Dame, IN: Christian Classics, 2010.

Jesus and the Last Things: Death, Judgment, Heaven, Hell. Eugene, OR: Wipf and Stock, 2019.

Jesus, the New Adam: Humanity's Steadfast Hope. Eugene, OR: Wipf and Stock, 2017.

Living in the Gap: Religious Life and the Call to Communion. Hyde Park, NY: New City Press, 2011; 2d ed., 2014.

Mary in 3-D: Icon of Discipleship, Doctrine, and Devotion. Hyde Park, NY: New City Press, 2015.

The Meaning of the Eucharist: Voices from the Twentieth Century. St. Louis, MO: En Route Books and Media, 2019.

Meeting Jesus on the Road to Emmaus: An Invitation to Friendship, Eucharist and Christian Community. New London, CT: Twenty-Third Publications, 2017.

The Mystery of the Eucharist: Voices from the Saints and Mystics. Hyde Park, NY: New City Press, 2014.

The "Our Father:" A Prayer's Power to Touch Hearts. Liguori, MO: Liguori Publications, 2012.

Plentiful Redemption: An Introduction to Alphonsian Spirituality. Liguori. MO: Liguori Publications, 2001.

Soliloquy Prayer: Unfolding Our Hearts to God. Liguori, MO: Liguori Publications, 1998.

Tending the Mustard Seed: Living the Faith in Today's World. Hyde Park, NY: New City Press, 2013.

Teresa of Avila, Interior Castle: Classic Text and Commentary. Notre Dame, IN: Christian Classics, 2007.

There Is a Season: Living the Liturgical Year. Liguori, MO: Liguori Publications, 2001.

Under the Starry Night: A Wayfarer's Guide through an Uncertain World. Notre Dame, IN: Ave Maria Press, 1997.

The Way of a Pilgrim: Complete Text and Reader's Guide. Liguori, MO: Liguori Publications, 2000.

www.ingramcontent.com/pod-product-compliance
Lightning Source LLC
Chambersburg PA
CBHW052107090426
42741CB00009B/1711